Why Saying Jesus Is A Jew Hurts Jews

Why Saying Jesus Is A Jew Hurts Jews

A Readable Examination of
Socio-Religious Factors

Nicholas Irish

The Hermit Kingdom Press
Cheltenham ♦ Seoul ♦ Bangalore ♦ Cebu

Why Saying Jesus Is A Jew Hurts Jews:
A Readable Examination of Socio-Religious Factors

Copyright © 2005 by Nicholas Irish

ISBN 1-59689-037-1 (paperback)
ISBN 1-59689-038-X (Adobe ebook)

(USA) Library of Congress Control Number: 2005923664

Write-To Address:

The Hermit Kingdom Press
3741 Walnut Street, Suite 407
Philadelphia, PA 19104
United States of America

Info@TheHermitKingdomPress.com

★ ★ ★ ★

Hermit Kingdom
12 South Bridge, Suite 370
Edinburgh, EH1 1DD
Scotland

http://www.TheHermitKingdomPress.com

In memory of
Corrie Ten Boon (1892-1983),
A devout Dutch Christian

Contents

"All forms of tampering with human beings, getting at them, shaping them against their will to your own pattern, all thought control and conditioning is, therefore, a denial of that in men which makes them men and their values ultimate."

Isaiah Berlin

HURT PRIDE

Saying that Jesus is a Jew hurts Jews because it hurts Christian pride. Saying that Jesus is a Jew may seem insignificant to those who are not Christians, but for many Christians this is a serious insult. There are several reasons why the pride of Christians is hurt by the statement. These reasons can be considered in a greater depth under these categories: (1) The belief that Jesus is God, (2) Historical experience of Christians, and (3) Group identity.

First, let's consider the Christian belief that Jesus is God and how this belief helps us understand why Christian pride is hurt when someone says that Jesus is a Jew.

Christians believe that Jesus Christ is God. In fact, it would not be wrong to say that the deity of Christ is fundamental to Christianity. In other words, Christianity would not be Christianity without the belief that Jesus Christ is God.

When we look at Christian history, it is filled with wars fought to defend the belief in the deity of Christ. Many Christians were killed because of the belief that Jesus Christ is God. In a sense, it would not be wrong to say that the whole history of Christianity is about the experience of believers in the deity of Jesus Christ.

Because Jesus Christ is central to Christianity, many Christian thinkers and preachers have expounded at length on the belief that Jesus Christ is God. In fact, Christian thinkers argue that both the Old Testament and the New Testament teach about Jesus Christ. They say that the Old Testament is prophetically looking forward to the coming of Jesus Christ, the Messiah. The New Testament accounts Jesus Christ's life on earth and the experience of the earliest Christians after the death and resurrection of Jesus Christ on earth. In every way, Jesus Christ is central to Christianity.

The belief in the deity of Jesus Christ is so central to Christianity that without it a person is not seen to be a Christian. In other words, a person who goes to church but refuses to believe that Jesus Christ is God is not considered a Christian. A person who does not believe in the deity of Christ cannot be baptized or allowed to participate in the Lord's Supper. In fact, it violates Christian Law for a clergy to baptize (or offer communion to) a person who refuses to acknowledge the deity of Christ. It is the profession that Jesus Christ is God that testifies to a person's identity as a Christian.

Because the belief in the deity of Jesus Christ has been so central to Christianity for thousands of years, even the most uneducated person attending church knows that this is an important belief in Christianity. In fact, the reason why a person is going to church is probably a testimony to his own personal position that Jesus Christ is God. Most likely, a person going to church has accepted Jesus Christ as God, personally.

In Christianity, various terms are used to refer to the process by which a person accepts Jesus Christ as God, personally. The most popular term to describe the process is "born again." A person is born again when he accepts Jesus Christ as God because the moment that he does, he is accepted as a child of God. Before being born again, he is merely a child of human parents, but after being born again, he is adopted as a child of God.

There are other terms to describe what happens when a person accepts in his heart that Jesus Christ is God. Beside the term "born again," Christians often use the term "justification." When a person accepts that Jesus Christ is God in his heart, he is justified.

What does it mean? It means that his sins are forgiven. Justification is a legal terminology. The Bible teaches us that all human beings are sinners because of original sin inherited at conception and the actual sin a person commits after being born from the mother's womb. The Bible also teaches that the wages of sin is death. In other words, in the court of God, all human beings deserve to die because of their sins. It is the just ruling in God's court. However, God sent His Son Jesus Christ (God the Word) to take on human flesh and die for us on the cross to bring forgiveness of sins.

Because of Jesus Christ's sacrificial death on the cross, there is a way to be forgiven of our sins. There is a way to avoid the death (eternal death) that is the righteous judgment of God – salvation comes by believing personally that Jesus Christ is the Savior God, the Messiah promised in the Old Testament and fulfilled in the New Testament. When a person believes that Jesus Christ is God, his sins are forgiven. In other words, the person's liability to suffer eternal death is taken away. In the court of God, the new believer is declared as righteous, or "justified," on the price of the blood of Jesus Christ on the cross. The new Christian believer is declared justified not on the merits of his righteousness, but on the merits of Christ's righteousness. Justification, as we can see, is a very important process. It gives us eternal life.

Justification is a legal terminology, but justification is basically the same as the term "born again." A person who is justified by the blood of Jesus Christ is born again by the grace of God.

Another term to refer to a person who personally accepts that Jesus Christ is God is "Christian convert." A person who believes in the deity of Christ has become a convert to Christianity. He has converted from his previous religion (or no religion) to the religion of Jesus Christ, as accounted in the Old Testament and the New Testament. A synonym for "convert" is "proselyte." Saying that a person is a Christian convert is the same as saying that a person is a Christian proselyte.

Whatever term we use (born again, justification, conversion, proselytized, child of God), we are referring to the same thing – a personal decision by a person to accept Jesus Christ as his personal God. Thus, it is easy to see why the deity of Jesus Christ is so important. Anyone who professes to being a Christian is implicitly saying that he has accepted Jesus Christ as his personal God. The deity of Jesus Christ is fundamental to Christianity and the Christian experience.

Seeing the importance of the divinity of Jesus Christ helps us to understand why denegration of the divinity of Jesus Christ can be deeply offensive.

When someone says that Jesus Christ is a Jew, it is basically implying that Jesus Christ is not God.

Logically, let's ask ourselves this question. Why would anyone call Jesus Christ a Jew? Why is it important to emphasize that Jesus is a Jew?

Most likely, when someone says that Jesus Christ is a Jew, he has a vested interest in the statement. For instance, he may be a Jew who wants to denegrate the divinity of Jesus Christ. Jews do not believe that Jesus Christ is God. By saying that Jesus Christ is a Jew, the person is making an implicit claim that Jesus Christ is not God.

It is not difficult to see why this is the case. When we say someone is a Jew, it often means that a person is religiously

Jewish. He may be a secular or liberal Jew, but he identifies in some way with the Jewish religion. So, a person says that Jesus is a Jew, he is in effect subsuming Jesus Christ under the authority of Judaism. In effect, that person is saying that Jesus Christ is not God but a follower of the Jewish religion.

This reality is clear when one reads any book on Jesus being a Jew. The fundamental principles in any book that claims that Jesus is a Jew will subsume Jesus under Jewish religion and law. This directly opposes Christianity.

Christians believe that Jesus Christ is God and under no human law. As God, Jesus Christ is the Creator of the World and the Supreme Sovereign Being. Yes, Jesus took on human flesh, but only to save us from our sins. He was sinless while being on earth. So, even with His human nature, it must be emphasized that Jesus Christ was God-Man with full divine status and divine power. To call Jesus Christ a Jew (or Roman or Greek, etc.) detracts from the fact of His divinity and his authority over all humans and all human laws. Yes, humans are influenced by human factors, but Jesus Christ isn't. He is God, even in his human flesh.

Calling Jesus a Jew pidgeonholes him into a category where He does not belong.

Although not all Christians can verbalize why it is wrong to call Jesus Christ a Jew fully, most Christians know that there is something wrong about it. The reason is that Christians believe that Jesus Christ is God. Calling Jesus Christ a Jew detracts from the central emphasis of Christianity without which Christianity is not Christianity.

In this light, it is easy to see why many Christians will take offense at the statement that Jesus Christ is a Jew. Even if some Christian leader wanted to push this idea, he will not be accepted by normal Christians in the street. Although a normal Christian in the street may not have read many academic books, he knows that the central factor in Christianity is that Jesus Christ is God. This belief is why he's a Christian. Because his belief is personal, a normal Christian in the street will most likely feel a deep personal offense at hearing that Jesus is a Jew.

Saying that Jesus is a Jew, therefore, will build resentment. It does not matter if it is said with the best of intentions. The statement is offensive by the very essence of the statement that denigrates the divinity of Jesus Christ and the apparent subsuming of Jesus Christ under the Jewish religion.

Saying that Jesus is a Jew will end up hurting Jews the most for this reason. Where will all the resentment finally go? If a Christian leader keeps emphasizing the idea that Jesus is a Jew and raises the ire of the normal Christian in the street, the ire will spill over. Most likely, the anger will not be directed at a fellow Christian. Rather, the resentment and anger will become focused on Jews.

There is a reason why the Holocaust happened in Germany when it did. The Holocaust came after a very important movement among some academic theologians in Germany that Jesus is a Jew. In academic circles, this trend is often described as The Quest of the Historical Jesus, often thought to be initiated by Albert Schweitzer (by the book by the same title) in the first decade of the 20th century, a couple of decades before Hitler came into power and only a few decades before the annihilation of Jews in Germany. Saying that Jesus is a Jew builds popular resentment, most often among normal Christian in the street, who has no interest in reading deep works of academic theology but who considers himself as a Christian.

Before the Holocaust, many describe academic theology in Germany as having gone far away from the popular Christian ethos of the German masses. In a type of Hegelian tragedy, the thesis imposed on theological study by academic theology found the antithesis of the German masses who felt personally insulted by calling Jesus Christ a Jew. The targets in the end were not fellow Christians (albeit academic theologians) but Jews (even Jewish neighbors) who lived in their midst.

The German case is not isolated. Calling Jesus a Jew has historically raised violent backlash from Christians who felt personally insulted because their primary identity as Christians was seen to be threatened and their God, the God of Christianity, subsumed under Judaism.

This leads into the next category of discussion – namely, the historical experience of Christians. It is because of the historical experience of Christians, that it can be said with confidence that calling Jesus a Jew will necessarily result in real harm coming to Jews. History is the proof.

Jews and Christians have had conflicts for a long-time. In fact, since the ministry of Jesus Christ on earth 2,000 years ago, Christians have experienced conflict with Jews. When Jews did not make incursions into Christianity to compel Christians to make concessions about the divinity of Christ or force Christians (either by influence or force) to state that Jesus is a Jew, Jews and Jewish communities lived in safety.

A good example is America. Jews in America have lived in relative peace, prosperity, and security because Jews in the past have not tried to force themselves into Christian discourse to belittle the deity of Christ or make Jesus Christ inferior to Judaism. There is no Christian church more emphatic about the deity of Christ than American Christian churches. Historically, there have been no Christian churches so militantly opposed to saying that Jesus is a Jew than American Christians. It is in this America that Jews have lived in safety and prosperity.

Unfortunately (for Jews), things have been changing. Many Jews are forcing themselves into academic discourse to emphasize that Jesus is a Jew. Even if some Christian academics emphasize that Jesus is a Jew, history shows that resentment will target Jews primarily. Resentment of normal Christian in the street is building. America is a country where if a Rabbi prays at a college graduation, many Christians often refuse to pray together. It is prohibited in historic Christianity to pray to any other God than the Trinity of Christianity. In a country with a clear Christian identity at all walks of life, any offensive efforts to push the agenda of Jesus being represented as a Jew will incur hatred (silent as it may be at first) of normal Christians in the street, who probably will not even read one book of academic theology in 10 years but who value Christianity and know what's in the Bible.

Only time will tell if violence against Jews will come as the result of the disturbing recent trends.

Historically, violence often came when Jews pushed their way into Christian religious spheres and pushed ideas that seemed to denigrate the divinity of Jesus Christ. Even if it is a Christian who aggressively push this idea, being influenced by a Jewish thinker, the ultimate expression of resentment (taking a few decades, perhaps) will be against Jews and Jewish communities.

A good example of this is Spain. In 1492 all Jews were expelled from Spain. A primary reason for the expulsion can be seen as the conflicts between Jews and Christians. Not unlike German Jews in Germany before the Holocaust who were running around in elite structures (there were more than a handful of Jews among German royals and the second in power in Weimar Republic was Jewish), many Spanish Jews were running around in elite structures. Like elite Jews before them, Jews in Spain who were academic and intellectual leaders made the mistake of forcing themselves into Christianity. There is a strong work of Jewish apologetics against Christianity coming from Spain. More important from the historical perspective, many elite Jewish intellectually directly engaged Christian thinkers in highly public cases whereby they flexed their intellectual and academic muscles to defeat Christian intellectuals and tried to compel Christians to adopt pro-Jewish positions.

A good example is the writings by Kimhi family from 12th to 13th centuries, trying to show that Christians should thank Jews for killing Jesus Christ. The basic argument is that since salvation is not possible without the death of Jesus Christ on the cross, Jews should be praised and thanked for killing Jesus Christ and making salvation possible for Christians. The writings of Kimhi had a profound impact on later Jewish writers and Jewish apologetic against Christians.

The fact that the expulsion of Jews from Spain in 1492 is directly tied to the perception that Jews were making incursions into Christianity and trying to subjugate Christianity under Judaism through influence and efficient inter-action is seen in the law expelling all Jews from Spain. Here is the second paragraph of the Edict of the Expulsion of the Jews (1492) that makes it clear that the issue was Jewish incursion into Christianity:

> *You know well or ought to know, that whereas we have been informed that in these our kingdoms there were some wicked Christians who Judaized and apostatized from our holy Catholic faith, the great cause of which was interaction between the Jews and these Christians, in the courts which we held in the city of Toledo in the past year of one thousand, four hundred and eighty,*

we ordered the separation of the said Jews in all the cities, towns and villages of our kingdoms and lordships and commanded that they be given Jewish quarters and separated places where they should live, hoping that by their separation the situation would remedy itself. Furthermore, we procured and gave orders that inquisition should be made in our aforementioned kingships and lordships, which as you know has for twelve years been made and is being made, and by many guilty persons have been discovered, as is very well known, and accordingly we are informed by the inquisitors and by other devout persons, ecclesiastical and secular, that great injury has resulted and still results, since the Christians have engaged in and continue to engage in social interaction and communication they have had means and ways they can to subvert and to steal faithful Christians from our holy Catholic faith and to separate them from it, and to draw them to themselves and subvert them to their own wicked belief and conviction, instructing them in the ceremonies and observances of

*their law, holding meetings at
which they read and teach that
which people must hold and
believe according to their law,
achieving that the Christians and
their children be circumcised, and
giving them books from which
they may read their prayers and
declaring to them the fasts that
they must keep, and joining with
them to read and teach them the
history of their law, indicating to
them the festivals before they
occur, advising them of what in
them they are to hold and observe,
carrying to them and giving to
them from their houses unlea-
vened bread and meats ritually
slaughtered, instructing them
about the things from which they
must refrain, as much in eating as
in other things in order to observe
their law, and persuading them as
much as they can to hold and
observe the law of Moses,
convincing them that there is no
other law or truth except for that
one. This proved by many
statements and confessions, both
from these same Jews and from
those who have been perverted
and enticed by them, which has
redounded to the great injury,*

*detriment, and opprobrium of our
holy Catholic faith.*

It is clear that that the issue was
influential, wealthy, and intellectual Jews
subverting Christianity and their being
effective. For such a law to be passed to
expel Jews (like laws being passed in
Germany to kill all Jews), there had to be
generally popular support, or at least lack
of explicit opposition to such laws being
passed. Because there was a long build-
up of resentment of normal people in the
street at what they saw as Jewish insult of
Christianity and Christians, there was
little public resistance to such laws.

In a sense, the more effective
Jews are, the more influential Jews are,
the more successful Jews are, the more
they invite violence against themselves.
This can be seen as the irony of Jewish
history. It is always at the strongest point
of Jewish history in any given country
that they meet their tragic end (such as in
Spain and Germany).

Historically, Jews were left alone
if they did not make aggressive incursions into Christianity and tried to force
Christians to adopt Jewish elements or
pro-Jewish practices or ideas, such as
saying that Jesus is a Jew. Of course, the

Spanish Jewish community was successful in getting their agenda into Christianity and among Christians because many Spanish Jews were very powerful politically, wealthy, well-educated, and in the most elite structures of the Spanish society. And it was their success that was their undoing, as it was the case in Germany. The success of Jews in winning intellectual battles with Christians or getting their pro-Jewish agenda through politics or society necessarily fuelled the growing resentment and inevitably invited violence inflicted on Jews and Jewish communities. This process was repeated again and again in the history of the west.

We can call this just as much a historical experience of the Jews as well as the historical experience of Christians. Certainly, what Christians experienced in terms of Jewish influences on Christianity almost always resulted in a popular backlash, backed up eventually by laws to expel or kill Jews. Resentment can be a scary thing. But it's understandable as a human experience – it is a part of human nature and history. Someone can fume and shout until he goes blue and say that it's not right. That doesn't change the fact that these things happened in history and will happen again. Just like German Jews in 1920 could never have envisioned what happened 20 years later, Spanish Jews could never have envisioned violence done against them because it appeared on the surface that they succeeded in getting people to become pro-Jewish explicitly and in the public forum.

Jews have lived in safety and in peace when they were weak as a community or when they refused to try to influence Christianity. But it seems like in history, whenever a Jewish community became strong, powerful, wealthy, and influential, conflicts emerged where Jewish muscle was flexed and Christianity impacted and altered to meet the pro-Jewish agenda. In the end, Jews necessarily suffered violence because resentment, invisible as it was, grew in a real way among the normal people in the street.

Thus, Christian history is an evidence that calling Jesus a Jew will build resentment and will necessarily bring down resentment against Jews and actual violence against Jews. The more successful Jews are, the more imminent the violence against Jews. This is simply a historic fact, based on the experience of

Jews and Christians in the west. Thus, visible victory is necessarily an actual defeat in this regard for Jews and Jewish communities.

It is not too difficult to see why this is the case. Group identity is a powerful social factor. I will discuss how group identity can enlighten why calling Jesus a Jew will end up in harm coming to Jews.

Christians comprise a group. Christians of all Christian denominations have the self-perception of being Christians. The group identity is bound by identity through Jesus Christ. Many Christians talk about having a personal relationship with Christ. Often, Christians talk about the family of Christ.

Perhaps more important than what Christians say are Christian practices. Christians are baptized and participate in the Lord's Supper (otherwise known as communion, mass, and eucharist). Christians pray to the Trinity. Christians celebrate common religious holidays (or holy days), such as Christmas and Easter. These factors bind Christians into a group. A Christian necessarily value these elements of Christianity, even if he does not necessarily observe all of the Christian practices actively, he values them in principle. Thus, he is a part of the group.

At the center of all Christian practices is Jesus Christ, the Christian God. For instance, Christmas is the celebration of the Incarnation of Jesus Christ ("God taking on human flesh" at birth in Bethlehem). Easter is the celebration of Jesus Christ from death on the cross, which is the evidence for His triumph over death.

Jesus Christ is also the center of Christian sacraments. Baptism is a celebration of being born again in Jesus Christ by accepting Him as one's personal God. The Lord's Supper is the celebration of the sacrificial death of Jesus Christ on the cross, which allowed forgiveness of sins and justification.

It is clear that Christianity and communal practices in Christianity focus on Jesus Christ and the belief that He is God. In other words, Christian group identity centers on the divinity of Jesus Christ. The fact that Jesus Christ is God is the most important factor in Christianity.

Because Christian group identity is bound up in the divinity of Jesus Christ, any efforts to downgrade this emphasis will produce resentment. If someone says that Jesus Christ is a Jew, the statement will fuel disgust and anger on the level of group identity.

This hostility can perhaps be better explained in terms of sports teams. For instance, if Chicago Cubs are playing Philadelphia Phillies in the World Series, you can be sure that Chicago residents are rooting for the Cubs and Philadelphia residents are rooting for the Phillies. If a Chicago resident comes to Philadelphia and starts to criticize the main pitcher for Phillies, many Philadelphians may resent him. In certain contexts in Philadelphia, it would not be surprising if he met some violence.

This is the case because there is group identity in operation. The fact that Philadelphians feel a group identity in reference to the city's baseball team makes them feel a certain way about the other team. Anger is raised when a member of the other team criticizes a key player of the Philadelphia's team.

This group identity operates on another level as well. If a Philadelphia resident starts extolling Chicago Cubs during the World Series, he will raise angers of Philadelphians present and invite violence. Many Philadelphians will call him a traitor and resent his pro-

Cubs position. Not all will resort to violence, but resentment will be present among most Philadelphians present for what they perceive as his betrayal of Philadelphia in the support of Chicago.

And it would not be surprising if the Philadelphians present will go out of their way to criticize Chicago Cubs. The reaction can be seen as a response. Whereas they may not have been hyper-critical, in the presence of perceived betrayal, the resentment will fuel an extreme attack on Chicago Cubs.

Group identity is important. Group identity impacts individual identity and human associations. Often, it is unspoken association that is just as real as water and oxygen.

In the same way, when someone starts calling Jesus a Jew, you will be perceived as criticizing the most important focus of Christianity. Many will perceive this as a slight and be offended by it. As a response, group identity will kick in and a more aggressive critical attitude toward Jews and Judaism will kick in. This is a natural group identity response. Whether it is sports group identity or religious group identity, there are similarities in socio-psychological dynamics.

The hostile group identity fuelled reaction to Judaism will be in effect whether a Jew calls Jesus a Jew or if a Christian calls Jesus a Jew. If a Jew calls Jesus a Jew, then those in the Christian group will perceive it as an attack of an outsider on the group. If a Christian calls Jesus a Jew, then those in the Christian group will see him as a traitor to the Christian group. Either way, the reaction will be hostility toward Judaism.

Calling Jesus a Jew is offensive to Christians because Christians believe that Jesus is God. Historically, there had been many conflicts, particularly with Jews, over the downgrading of the status of Jesus Christ and His teachings, which are directly opposed to Jewish ritual regulations, as attested in the New Testament. Group identity is just a part of being a human being, living and associating in society. Christian group identity will play a role when someone calls Jesus a Jew.

Simply put, it is not a good idea to call Jesus a Jew. It attacks what is most important in Christianity – the divinity of Jesus Christ. Calling Jesus a Jew attacks Christians on an individual and personal levels because becoming

Christian meant accepting Jesus Christ as the personal God, who saves.

Calling Jesus Christ a Jew hurts Christian pride on individual and group levels. It is the kind of injury to pride that breeds contempt and fuels resentment. Anger and resentment can naturally lead to violence, generally directed at Jews, regardless of who said Jesus is a Jew. History provides many examples of this.

It may help to examine the Bible more in depth to see why calling Jesus a Jew is a very big insult for Christians on individual and group levels.

BIBLICAL TEACHING

Saying that Jesus is a Jew is deeply offensive to Christians. Many Christians feel that the statement attacks their individual identity and group identity as Christians. Some feel that the statement is not only an insult to them personally but also an insult against the Word of God.

Christians believe that the Bible is the Word of God. The Christian Bible is composed of the Old Testament and the New Testament. Christians believe that the Old Testament was given primarily to prophesy about Jesus Christ. In other words, the Old Testament prepared people to welcome Jesus Christ to earth.

The New Testament represents the fulfilment of the prophecies in the Old Testament. The Gospels (Matthew, Mark, Luke, and John) record the life and ministry of Jesus Christ on earth. All the Gospels emphasize that Jesus Christ is the fulfilment of the law and the pro-phecies of the Old Testament.

The portions of the New Testa-ment describing the events after the ascension of Jesus Christ to Heaven focus on Jesus Christ. One cannot read the writings of divinely inspired writer St. Paul without finding his focus falling on Jesus Christ, time and time again.

Indeed, after the Incarnation of Jesus Christ, Christians focus on Jesus Christ, who is God who came down to earth in order to die a sacrificial death for sinners to procure eternal life for them.

The first chapter of the Gospel according to John is one of the most visible evidence that the Bible emphasizes that Jesus Christ is God. Gospel of John 1:1-5 states:

> *In the beginning was the Word, and the Word was with God, and the Word was God. He was with God in the beginning. Through him all things were made; without him nothing was made that has been made. In him was life, and that life was the light of men. The light shines in the darkness, but the darkness has not understood it.*

It is clear here that the Word is God. And we also see here the formula for the Trinity. The Word is God. But the Word is also with God.

In the Nicene Creed, one of the historic Christian confessions recited by the Christian community, like the Apostle's Creed, emphasizes that there are three "persons" in God: God the Father, God the Son, and God the Holy Spirit. They are separate persons but all are one God. If you haven't read the Nicene Creed, it may be worthwhile to go back and study that as it is very important in Christianity.

But even without the Nicene Creed, we see the principle of the Trinity here. The Word was with God and the Word is God. Separate but one, like the principle of the Trinity as outlined in the Nicene Creed. The Gospel of John does a good job explaining the situation.

The Word as God was involved in the creation of the world. Thus, the Word can be seen as the Creator God who created as recorded in the Book of Genesis.

The Gospel of John emphasizes the divine attributes of the Word. In Word is life. The Word as the source of life is the master of all living, created order.

Who is this Word, who is God? The Gospel of John is clear in showing that Jesus Christ is the Word. Gospel of John 1:14-17 states:

The Word became flesh and made his dwelling among us.

We have seen his glory, the glory of the One and Only, who came from the Father, full of grace and truth. John testifies concerning him. He cries out, saying, "This was he of whom I said, 'He who comes after me has surpassed me because he was before me.'" From the fullness of his grace we have all received one blessing after another. For the law was given through Moses; grace and truth came through Jesus Christ.

The Gospel of John clearly emphasizes that Jesus Christ is God because John wanted all Christians to be certain about this Biblical Truth.

The fact that Jesus Christ is God is foundational to Christianity. It is, in essence, the most important belief for all Christians. The divinity of Jesus Christ is what makes Christianity Christianity. It is the essence of the Christian faith.

Because Jesus Christ is God and this idea is continuously emphasized in the Bible, when a Christian hear someone trying to emphasize that Jesus is a Jew, he is more likely than not to become very angry. Most Christians would consider it blasphemous to call Jesus Christ a Jew.

One of the reasons why many Christians find it deeply offensive to hear someone call Jesus Christ a Jew is that the Bible emphasizes that Jews killed Jesus Christ. Gospel of John 19:11-16 attributes guilt for Jesus Christ's death directly to Jews:

> *Jesus answered, "You would have no power over me if it were not given to you from above. Therefore the one who handed me over to you is guilty of a greater sin." From then on, Pilate tried to set Jesus free but the Jews kept shouting, "If you let this man go, you are no friend of Caesar. Anyone who claims to be a king opposes Caesar." When Pilate heard this, he brought Jesus out and sat down on the judge's seat at a place known as the Stone Pavement (which in Aramaic is Gabbatha). It was the day of Preparation of Passover Week, about the sixth hour. "Here is your king," Pilate said to the Jews. But they shouted, "Take*

> *him away! Take him away!*
> *Crucify him!" "Shall I crucify*
> *your king?" Pilate asked. "We*
> *have no king but Caesar," the*
> *chief priests answered. Finally,*
> *Pilate handed him over to them*
> *to be crucified.*

What is clear in this passage in the Gospel of John is that Pilate, the Roman authority tried to free Jesus Christ. It is the Jews who prevented His release. It is the Jews who forced Jesus Christ into being killed. In fact, Pilate handed Jesus Christ over to the Jews to be killed. The Gospel of John is clear about the guilt of Jews in the murder of Jesus Christ. In essence, Romans are exonerated and the Jews are shown to be guilty.

The intention to kill Jesus Christ was always with the Jews. Elite Jews decide in an official meeting of elite Jews that they need to kill Jesus Christ. The account of the decision in the Sanhedrin is recorded in Gospel of John 11. Elite Jews make a plot to kill Jesus Christ in an official meeting of the governing body of the Jews. Jesus Christ was not even present at the Jewish high court. But the absence of Jesus Christ did not matter. The Jews wanted to have Jesus Christ killed and so Jesus Christ was found to be guilty without a trial and a sentence against him was passed without Jesus Christ being allowed to offer up his defense in the Jewish high court.

But it is not merely the elite Jews who try to kill Jesus Christ. Jewish masses try to kill Jesus Christ on more than one occasion. One account of Jewish masses trying to kill Jesus Christ can be found in Gospel of John 10:22-33. The part of this passage that is most enlightening is found in Gospel of John 10:31-33:

> *Again the Jews picked up stones to stone him, but Jesus said to them, "I have shown you many great miracles from the Father. For which of these do you stone me?" "We are not stoning you for any of these," replied the Jews, "but for blasphemy, because you, a mere man, claim to be God."*

The Jewish masses tried to kill Jesus Christ because Jesus Christ was proclaiming that He is God. Jews did not want to accept Jesus Christ as God and so they wanted to kill Him. Jews trying to kill Jesus Christ is one of the central themes of the Gospels.

Because the Bible is emphatic about the fact that Jews tried to kill Jesus Christ and finally succeeded in the evil deed, many Christians find it deeply offensive when someone says that Jesus Christ is a Jew.

It is not merely because Jews are Christ-killers that Christians find it offensive when someone, particularly a Jew, says that Jesus is a Jew. The Bible portrays Jews in the most negative terms. In fact, Jesus Christ Himself taught that Jews are evil.

It is no surprise for anyone who has read the Bible that Jesus Christ constantly attacks Jews and Jewish prayer. In fact, Jesus Christ disliked Jewish prayers so much that He taught His disciples the Lord's Prayer, to oppose Jewish prayers.

Jesus Christ describes Jews as keeping the laws of the Old Testament for its own sake. They miss the point that the Old Testament was pointing to Jesus Christ. It made no sense to keep regulations for the sake of keeping regulations and miss the point that Jesus Christ is the fulfilment of the law.

Jesus Christ was so disgusted with Jews that He went around condemning Jewish laws. Jesus Christ publicly defied Jewish purity laws and intentionally offended Jewish leaders. Jesus Christ called Himself the Lord of the Sabbath, clearly making the claim that He is God. Jews did not miss the point and wanted to kill Jesus Christ.

Not only did Jesus Christ publicly condemn Jewish laws, He publicly attacked Jews. In the Gospel of John 8, Jesus Christ calls Jews the children of the devil. The Bible shows that this anti-Jewish slur was not meant to be haphazard or superficial. Jesus Christ launches a long tirade regarding how Jews are the children of the devil. Jesus Christ elaborates on how Jews are evil. Thus, calling Jews the children of the devil is a part of Jesus Christ's sermon against the Jews in a heated anti-Jewish invective.

Jesus Christ did not merely show his disgust at Jews verbally. Jesus Christ was physically violent. One time, Jesus Christ entered a Jewish place of worship and started to destroy everything and disturb peace and order. Gospel of Mark 11:15-16 describes:

> *On reaching Jerusalem, Jesus entered the temple area and began driving out those who were buying and selling there. He overturned the tables of the money changers and the benches of those selling doves, and would not allow anyone to carry merchandise through the temple courts.*

The merchants had the legal right to be there. They were facilitating Jewish religious sacrifice by providing animals for sacrifice required by Judaism at the time. Jesus Christ used violence to show His condemnation of and disdain for the Jewish religion. Jewish sacrifices in Jesus Christ's mind were useless. The Jews should have accepted Jesus Christ as God and should have been praying to God.

The Jews understood that Jesus Christ had a disdain for Jews and Judaism. In the Gospel of Mark 11:18, we see that Jewish religious leaders plot to kill Jesus Christ. Jesus Christ considered Judaism and Jewish practices as evil, and the Jews hated Jesus Christ and sought to murder Him.

The conflict between Jews and Christians was at the earliest stages of Jesus Christ's ministry on earth. Jesus Christ constantly fought with Jews, primarily because Jews refused to accept Jesus Christ as God. Jesus Christ is the Word, who is God. It was in His love and mercy that Jesus Christ came to earth to save human beings, including Jews. All humans have to do is to accept that Jesus Christ is God in thanksgiving. But most Jews refused to do that. Not only that Jews organized to kill Jesus Christ. This is why Jesus Christ calls Jews the children of the devil.

The conflict between Christians and Jews continued after the ascension of Jesus Christ to Heaven. In fact, we read of the prominent case of St. Stephen getting stoned to death by Jews in the Book of Acts 7. Jews organized people systematically in order to kill Christians. Pharisees ran around trying to arrest or kill Christians. Saul the Pharisee used to be one of these zealous for the Jewish religion, until he was converted into Christianity.

After his conversion, St. Paul spent his lifetime fighting Judaism and Jews who tried to infiltrate Christianity and taint Christianity with Jewish influences. St. Paul follows Jesus Christ in emphasizing that Judaism and Christianity are fundamentally opposi-tional. There is nothing in common be-tween Christianity and Judaism because the central pillar of Christianity is that Jesus is God. Judaism rejects this funda-mental principle.

Christians believe that the Old Testament is about Jesus Christ. Judaism never accepted this position and never will. Thus, Christianity and Judaism are fundamentally opposed to each other.

The Bible is clear in drawing a line between Judaism and Christianity. Because of the Biblical teaching about Jews and Judaism, it is understandable why many Christians actually start fum-ing when someone, especially if they are Jews, start calling Jesus Christ a Jew. It makes logical and historical sense.

POLITICS

Not surprisingly politics plays a role. Saying that Jesus is a Jew creates both political opportunism and political agenda. Interestingly enough, saying that Jesus is a Jew almost inevitably hurts Jews and Jewish groups. This may be ironic in light of the fact that Jewish groups often presume at the start that saying that Jesus is a Jew helps Jews and Jewish groups. Let us unpack the thinking on the Jewish side first.

Many Jews may feel that it is logical that if they claim that Jesus is a Jew that people who are not Jewish will feel an affinity to them. Jews may think: Is it not like saying that I'm from England? Don't all English people feel a type of group identity by the virtue of the fact that they have a shared group identity?

On the surface, this rationale seems to make sense. When there is an Olympic game and England is playing against France, it seems natural that all people who think of themselves as English would cheer against France. There is a shared sentiment and identity with the factor of "English" in common.

So, some Jews may presume: Is it not the case with saying that Jesus is a Jew? All who share an identity attached to being a follower of Jesus Christ will feel a sense of kinship with Jews if it is emphasized that Jesus is a Jew.

The problem with this assumption, of course, is understandable in light of previous chapters. Christian self-understanding and group identity is pre-figured against Judaism and Jewish identity. The New Testament places Christianity against Judaism. In fact, the New Testament emphasizes that Jews killed Jesus Christ. Historically, Christians have preserved the ethos of this understanding of Jesus Christ's life and death.

Thus, while it may seem logical that saying that Jesus is a Jew will endear Christians to Jews, it can have the opposite effect. The New Testament is a written document and in plain sight for all to see and read. There is the historical experience that ingrains certain under-standing as "common knowledge" that pervades society at the lowest common denominator. Although there may be a few who may be won over, most will not be.

In fact, emphasizing that Jesus is a Jew will have the opposite effect of reminding Christians of the New Testa-ment teaching against Jews and puffing up historical prejudices against Jews.

The upshot is that emphasizing that Jesus is a Jew will hurt Jews.

Thus, whereas if the Jews left the issue alone – or "silent" – then Christians would not have been reminded of the conflict between Christians and Jews, because Jews emphasize this point, Christian resentment and awareness are raised.

What does this mean politically? It is possible that some Jews emphasize that Jesus is a Jew out of political opportunism. These Jews may think that it will help them get Christian votes and Christian political support.

Some Jews may have a political agenda. They may want to divide Christian votes in half. These Jews may want to use the Jesus-as-a-Jew idea as a type of divide and conquer methodology. There may be a political agenda to gain a political positioning and dominance.

It is possible that this strategy may work at first or for a while. However, for the reasons already given, this strategy is doomed to failure. Anti-Jewish polemic is an integral and even essential part of Christianity and the history of Christians for the past two thousand years. Anti-Judaism, therefore, is engrained in the culture and is internalized in the individual psyche. The anti-Jewish expression, although not explicit or overt, is always implicit and internally assumed.

As this anti-Judaism pervades through the society at every level and is reminded of by many essential cultural artefacts and experiences – both living and historically remembered – it cannot be wiped out. Even conscious efforts to destroy anti-Jewish sentiment is doomed to failure because every individual is a carrier of the historical hatred, more internalized than external.

In other words, anti-Jewish phenolmena is historical and integral to western experience. In a sense, anti-Jewish perception or outlook is a part of what people are as individuals and as a group.

Thus, it is not surprising that when one says, "Jew," people have a perception of what Jews are. A westerner hearing the word "Jew" will think that Jews are stingy. This perception goes all the way back to the Middle Ages when Jews were hated for practicing usury. Of course, many westerners will not think consciously of the practice of usury by Jews in the Middle Ages when they think about Jews as "money grubbing, stingy people." But the attachment that Jews naturally have with money is historical.

Of course, the fact that one of the most influential banking families – if not the most influential – even today is the Jewish family of Rothchilds does not help to dispel the notion that Jews are usurious and "tight with money."

But even without the Rothchilds and many Jewish individuals involved in the financial and banking sectors, perceptions of Jews as money-loving characters who have no scruples or morals exist. This perception about Jews is internalized in the western culture.

This is nowhere more evident than in western literature. The image of Jews as usurious and unprincipled money-sharks exist throughout the whole gamut of western literature. Take for instance *The Merchant of Venice*. It is a play written by William Shakespeare several hundred years ago. It portrays Jews as usurious and celebrating at the financial misfortune of others. The most recent movie made about the play in 2004 with Al Pacino as the Jewish Shylock is faithful to the negative portrayal of Jews as leeches that are detrimental to the weal of society. Jews stand for all that is evil in a community.

One can argue that people in Hollywood who made the movie were merely being faithful to the original play of Shakespeare. However, there are several factors to consider. First, why did the producers decide to make this movie? There are a lot of Shakespearean plays out there that they could have chosen. Why this one knowing that the whole play celebrates the destruction of Jews? Second, why did Al Pacino take the part, knowing that Shylock is the symbol of the Jew hated in Europe? Al Pacino gave "street credit" to the movie by adding his famous persona to the movie. And Al Pacino plays the part expertly in a way that the audience comes to hate Shylock the Jew. Thirdly, why was this movie made and released in 2004? The movie people knew that this movie would offend Jews.

Perhaps the last point is the most insightful in understanding the political factor under discussion. The movie was released in 2004 because the people who produced the movie believed that the movie will make money in 2004. In other words, despite the political correctness culture, the producers and movie studio felt that there is enough anti-Jewish sentiment in the world to make this movie a financial success. The perception is very important.

It is interesting that in 2004, Mel Gibson's *The Passion of the Christ* was released. This is also a movie that portrays Jews negatively. The movie depicts Jews as Christ-killers. Of course, this is a faithful rendering of the New Testament account of the crucifixion.

Similar questions can be raised. Mel Gibson is an artist but also a businessman. Gibson did not make the movie to lose money. Why did Mel Gibson think that this movie would make money?

Mel Gibson knew that there are billions of Christians around the world. There is a ready market for a movie that faithfully portrays the New Testament. And he was right. The movie made hundreds of millions of dollars more than the most generous estimates by experts in the movie industry.

Mel Gibson correctly read the market – if we are to talk in terms of supply and demand economics of capitalism.

Of course, I am not denying that Mel Gibson made the movie as a personal Christian testimony. Mel Gibson is a devout Christian who believes in historic Christianity and its value for the world. It doesn't hurt that there are billions out there who agree with him essentially. Mel Gibson was able to make a testimony of his faith and make hundreds of millions of dollars in the process.

In light of our current discussion, it is important to point out that the negative perception of Jews in the movie (and in the New Testament!) should be seen as normative for most of the billions who call themselves Christians. Jews may find the portrayal offensive or disturbing, but the majority of Christians have absolutely no problem with it.

Politically, this is significant. Shrewd politicians who are in tune with the cultural trends and the innate perception of the people will understand that Jews are generally not well-liked by the people.

Political opportunists will learn to use this to their advantage. Knowing that Jews are not well-liked by the populace, those who want to gain a political edge will point to negative portrayals of Jews. They know that they will get more votes by playing up anti-Jewish sentiment, either explicitly or in a more subtle manner.

When Jews emphasize that Jesus was a Jews, they play into the hands of political opportunism. The very fact of emphasizing brings the issue of Jewishness out into the open. It is a way that the populace are reminded about "the Jewish conspiracy." Even if Jews intend to benefit themselves by the emphasis, they should not forget that people have internalized perception of Jews. This has been historically conditioned over 2,000 years. And integral to the perception is that Jews conspired to kill Jesus Christ. The New Testament is a proof-positive for many that there is a Jewish conspiracy. And the thought would go that if there was a Jewish conspiracy once, there would be Jewish conspiracy again. When Jews say that Jesus is a Jew, this feeds into the internalized perception by non-Jews that Jews are always conspiring.

The Jewish conspiracy theory works well for political opportunists opposing Jews. Ironically, Jews emphasizing that Jesus is a Jew has a long-term effect of helping those who are political enemies of Jewish candidates or Jewish groups.

Even if it were "Christians" who emphasized that Jesus is a Jew, it would help "the enemy of the Jews." Why? It is because historical hatred never really dies. It becomes minimized or maximized at times but it always exists. It is internalized in the culture and in individual and group identities, particularly in the western context.

It does not matter what the intention of these "Christians" is. Maybe there are Judas Ischariots who want to betray Christianity and that is why they say that Jesus is a Jew. It is possible that some actually believe that Jesus is a Jew and it is an important factor to emphasize. It doesn't matter what the reason is. The fact is it is impossible to wipe out 2,000 years of history and cultural programming, which have more often than not been effectuated through passive process in experience rather than active inculcation.

Take for instance the Christian season of Lent. When the Gospel portions detailing the suffering and death of Jesus Christ is read, it is impossible to avoid the negative portrayal of Jews in the New Testament. It is a part of the historical experience and the New Testament cannot be rewritten.

Whether people who say Jesus is a Jew say it with good intentions or bad, the end result is that it will create discontentment. People can read the New Testament for themselves. They can see for themselves what the Jews did to Jesus Christ. They can read that Jews persecuted Jesus Christ and tried to manipulate the legal system to have Jesus Christ killed.

The more that the idea that Jesus is a Jew is emphasized the more people will be incited to hate the Jews. Whereas they would not have been reminded about Jewish complicity in the murder of Jesus, the very fact that the offensive statement is uttered adds salt to the sore that they did not think much about.

Thus, political opportunists can utilize heightened sense of ill feeling towards Jews to gain a political edge.

There may be proactive political agenda created as a result of some people emphasizing that Jesus is a Jew. There may be a systematic political agenda to disenfranchise the Jews from political power and social influence. Politicians may do this as an active political agenda out of their personal Christian faith or Christian commitments.

But it is also possible that the purpose may not be as noble. There are politicians who hate Jews. They may not say it, but they do. This should not be surprising in light of the historical experience of the west. It would be more natural than not for a person in the west to hate Jews given the 2,000 years of western history. Of course, they may never admit it – even to themselves – but it is an invariable part of their identity and perception as a member of the western society, culturally programmed over 2,000 years.

Thus, politicians who hate Jews – whether consciously or subconsciously – can aid in a political agenda against the Jews. This agenda would be fuelled by the statement that Jesus is a Jew. It can be like a trigger of anger or discontent.

Perhaps more significant than what politicians do or feel is what the populace feels and does. Just as saying that Jesus is a Jew can be a trigger for non-Jewish politicians in the west, it can trigger the non-Jewish populace. Thus, non-Jews may develop a type of political agenda to oppose the Jews. This can be on a conscious or a subconscious level. It can be proactive or more passive in nature. It can be systematic or sponta-neous. It can be peaceful or violent. Whatever the precise nature of the combustible political agenda against Jews among the populace, it will have the end result of hurting Jews in all kinds of ways.

Of course, political agenda against Jews by the populace is far more damaging to the Jews than that by a person in politics. With the populace, damage control is far more difficult and may be impossible.

Some examples of political agenda against Jews that go from ground up are found in the pogroms in Russia. Violent acts against Jews erupted all over and often spontaneously. There was no way to control it. Certainly, the pogroms against Jews in Russia are not isolated or confined to the 19th and 20th centuries. Violent acts against Jews have occurred in different cultures and in various countries throughout 2,000 years. And certainly, such acts can happen in the next 2,000 years as well.

Pogroms were almost exclusively initiated by the populace. It is possible to call the pogroms, "popular political agenda against the Jews." However, what is more likely in history is not a political combustion against the Jews by the people or exclusively among politicians but a combination of the two. There is often a meeting of the minds in political agenda against the Jews –

whether proactively or more passively –
among the non-Jewish politicians and the
non-Jewish voting public. The process
can be systematic, logical, and traceable.
However, the process of political agenda
against Jews can just as well be
spontaneous, untraceable, haphazard, and
out-of-the-blue.

Saying that Jesus is a Jew can be
the trigger that creates, prods, facilitates,
or pushes the process of political agenda
against the Jews. Needless to say, saying
that Jesus is a Jew hurts the Jews.

SOCIAL JEALOUSY

There is another important reason why saying that Jesus is a Jew hurts Jews. This reason can be entitled, "social jealousy." This chapter will explain what social jealousy is and how it relates to the statement that Jesus is a Jew.

Perhaps, social jealousy can be better understood from some examples. Let's say that there is a person named Peter and another person named Mark. Peter goes to Mark and says he is better than Mark. What would be the immediate response? Mark would be upset and may express his anger at Peter. Why is Mark angry at Peter? It can be explained as "social jealousy." Peter has told Mark that he is better than him. Mark feels upset because he is experiencing social jealousy at the statement uttered. It is not important whether the statement is true or not. The mere fact that the statement is uttered makes Mark feel social jealousy. This jealousy engenders a reaction in Mark against Peter.

Take another example. Let's say that Peter has just purchased a Mercedes Benz. Mark drives a midsized car that is a nice car but not in the expensive category. Peter goes to Mark and tells Mark how good his car is and how much he likes his car. Mark feels upset and may even hate Peter for saying this. Why? It is because Mark feels social jealousy against Peter. Where did this social jealousy come from? It came from the claim by Peter that his car is better than Mark's car. It may be a fact. But that is besides the point. It is the very fact that Peter "rubbed it in" that caused Mark to feel particularly angry and even hate Peter.

The two examples illustrate an important factor about social jealousy. Social jealousy is based on a claim of superiority by an individual. It is irrelevant whether it is factual or not. In a sense, the claim relates in some way to an assertion of social superiority, either on account of what a person has or what he is or what he has accomplished. Social jealousy is exacerbated when the person (Peter in the examples) repeat again and again his superiority over another person (Mark in the examples).

In the same way, when Jews claim that Jesus is a Jew, they are asserting a type of social superiority over non-Jews. It is like Peter saying that his Mercedes is better than Mark's car. Just as that is actually saying that Peter is better than Mark (and Mark will perceive it in that way), claiming that Jesus is a

Jew is like saying that Jews are superior to non-Jews. Most non-Jews will not miss the point. It is not important whether the statement is true or not. Non-Jews will feel social jealousy over the claim to social superiority in the statement that Jesus is a Jew. Thus, adverse reaction against Jews – even hatred against Jews – will naturally follow.

It is possible to understand the force of social jealousy when we understand how human beings are wired. Jealousy on any level is a powerful force. People do all kinds of evil on account of jealousy. In the book of Genesis, the first murder was on account of jealousy. Cain killed Abel because Cain's sacrifice was not accepted but Abel's was. David had Bethsheba's husband killed after committing adultery with her because he was jealous. David was jealous of Bethsheba's husband for being her husband so he basically had him killed. Then, David married Bethsheba. Of course, the Bible condemns violent acts of jealous rage. However, the Bible also recognizes it as a part of human nature.

In life situations, it is not difficult to see how jealousy functions. Friends often betray their closest friend because they are jealous. The Germans even have a saying for celebrating the misfortune of a close one – Schadenfreude. This is the other side of the coin of jealousy. Whereas one feels anger when one feels jealousy, one feels joy when one sees misfortune of those whom they are jealous about. Who knows? Maybe this partly explains the Holocaust?

Jealousy makes people do all kinds of things against others. Jealousy is not only a feeling but a feeling that often spurs action.

Thus, it is not surprising to see how social jealousy against Jews on account of the claim that Jesus is a Jew can hurt Jews. People can be driven to violence against Jews, fuelled by their social jealousy. It is irrelevant if the claim is true or false. The very fact of the claim is enough to raise social jealousy which may potentially result in violent action against Jews.

This is not only the case when Jews claim that Jesus is a Jew. Even if a third-party claims that Jesus is a Jew, it is sure to raise social jealousy. This is not difficult to see if one sees what happens in his own life.

Let's say that someone starts saying that Peter is far better than Mark in his job. What will happen? Mark will be upset at the person who makes that statement but he will certainly hate Peter. And it's not just Mark. If a boss kept praising how brilliant Peter is at his job, all of his co-workers will feel social jealousy towards Peter. It's not important whether the statement is true or not. The very fact that the claim to social superiority of Peter is made is enough to engender social jealousy against Peter.

The same is true when someone claims that Peter's car is better than Mark's. Mark may be upset at the person who made the statement but he is bound to be far more resentful towards Peter. If the superiority of Peter's car is emphasized in group settings, Peter is sure to experience fallout from social jealousy experienced by his group.

It is easy to see why saying that Jesus is a Jew will hurt Jews even when a non-Jew says it. It doesn't matter if the statement is true or not. Social jealousy will most probably propel non-Jews toward hatred of Jews.

It is not surprising how this works. When we examine acts of violence against Jews throughout history, often they were done when the Jewish communities were highly successful. When Jews are enjoying privilege and prosperity, they are often the most vulnerable. That is because social jealousy can be a motivating factor for hatred and violent attacks.

Claiming that Jesus is a Jew operates on the same level. Whether the statement is true or false is irrelevant. The very claim is enough to engender social jealousy that engineers hatred and potential violence.

Claiming that Jesus is a Jew is a very bad idea. It can effectuate violence against Jews. Certainly, social jealousy is attached to the fact that Jesus Christ is very personal to many people around the world. Every Christian accepts Jesus Christ as God and personal LORD and Savior.

Because Jesus Christ is very personal, that makes any claim to Jesus very personal. People are bound to take things very personally and it is completely understandable.

Given the historical experience, the New Testament, and human nature, it is easy to see why saying that Jesus is a Jew hurts Jews.

Of course, if one is Jewish, he should be more concerned that the claim that Jesus is a Jew is discouraged. The claim can actually affect him adversely.

It is possible that claiming that Jesus is a Jew can put the ball in motion for eventual violence against Jews – and even murder of Jews, like in the Holocaust.

For Christians, those who are concerned about the truth claim of the New Testament, they would want to discourage the statement that Jesus is a Jew. Furthermore, Christians who oppose and discourage the statement that Jesus is a Jew in times of peace can be doing Jews a favor for the future when times may not be so peaceful.

About the Author

Nicholas Irish is a well-read intellectual who has travelled widely around the world. Irish draws his insights from his historical research, personal observation, and experience. He lives alone in Europe always thinking about the meaning of life and the phenomena of human experience.

www.ingramcontent.com/pod-product-compliance
Lightning Source LLC
LaVergne TN
LVHW011215080426
835508LV00007B/795